Sites and Bites
Volume 1

Michelle Fedosoff

First published by Ultimate World Publishing 2024
Copyright © 2024 Michelle Fedosoff

ISBN

Paperback: 978-1-923255-23-4
Ebook: 978-1-923255-24-1

Michelle Fedosoff has asserted her rights under the Copyright, Designs and Patents Act 1988 to be identified as the author of this work. The information in this book is based on the author's experiences and opinions. The publisher specifically disclaims responsibility for any adverse consequences which may result from use of the information contained herein. Permission to use information has been sought by the author. Any breaches will be rectified in further editions of the book.

All rights reserved. No part of this publication may be reproduced, stored in or introduced into a retrieval system, or transmitted in any form, or by any means (electronic, mechanical, photocopying, recording or otherwise) without the prior written permission of the author. Any person who does any unauthorized act in relation to this publication may be liable to criminal prosecution and civil claims for damages. Enquiries should be made through the publisher.

Cover design: Ultimate World Publishing
Layout and typesetting: Ultimate World Publishing
Editor: Rebecca Low

Ultimate World Publishing
Diamond Creek,
Victoria Australia 3089
www.writeabook.com.au

Testimonials

As a fellow traveler, I found myself deeply relating to all of Michelle's stories. From the chaotic flights to the enchanting destinations, her vivid descriptions made me feel as though I was right there with her. In *'Sites and Bites,'* Michelle's engaging humour and fun-loving style captivate readers, making the book a delightful read. The short stories of her family adventures around the globe transform this book into a little gem. I highly recommend it to anyone who enjoys armchair travel and seeks inspiration for their next adventure.

Vivienne Mason – Author

If you've ever found yourself lost in an unfamiliar city, unsure of your next move, this book is for you. Michelle perfectly captures the essence of travel mishaps, transforming potential disasters into laugh-out-loud moments. From missing flights to unexpected detours, every story highlights the humour in the chaos of travel. This book reminds us that life, much like travel, is unpredictable, and that's exactly what makes it an adventure. It's a must-read for anyone who loves to travel or simply enjoys a good laugh. Embrace the unexpected and find joy in the journey!

Julie Fisher – Author

Sites and Bites
Volume 1

SHORT TRAVEL STORIES FOR YOUR ENJOYMENT

I remember listening to a friend of mine who was talking about his latest trip to Mexico. He said it was the worst trip of his life. The weather was stormy, cold, and windy, so hanging out at the beach wasn't an option. He also talked about the good food he had eaten and the fun entertainment at the resort, but in his mind, it was still the worst trip ever.

That got me thinking. Like most people I know, I have high expectations when I travel, most likely because I spend so much time thinking about it before I go. But when I started to really think about the trips I've taken, they rarely went 100% as planned.

Does that make it a bad trip, though? I suppose you could think of it that way, but I choose to think that these bumps in the trip are what make the best stories.

Contents

Testimonials	iii
Short Travel Stories for Your Enjoyment	v
Chapter 1: Following Rick Steves' Advice	1
Chapter 2: Taj Mahal Tourist Attraction	13
Chapter 3: Scary Plane Ride	21
Chapter 4: Where Are My Socks?	31
Chapter 5: Wedding Crasher in Vancouver	37
Chapter 6: Family Christmas in Manzanillo	43
Chapter 7: Cinque Terre Sleepover	51
Chapter 8: Beary Scary	59
Chapter 9: Pig Snout Drama	73
Chapter 10: Cocolalla Cabin	79
Chapter 11: Las Vegas Baby	87
Chapter 12: Bikinis and Socks in Hawaii	95
Chapter 13: Breakfast at Pepe's	103
Chapter 14: Truck Stop Sleepover	107
Chapter 15: Road Trip with a Stranger	111
The End	119
Acknowledgements	121
About the Author	123

CHAPTER 1

Following Rick Steves' Advice

My husband Greg and I are both huge fans of Rick Steves. We have spent years organizing our evening schedule around watching his travel programs. I've enjoyed learning about new places, and his programs made me realize there was a different way to travel than booking hotel rooms and tour packages.

One evening, my husband and I were watching an episode of *Rick Steves' Europe Through the Back Door*, and we decided we were going to book a trip to Europe and do it the Rick Steves way: pack light, find good-value accommodations, and connect with locals.

The next day, I booked vacation time for the following spring, and the research began. Where did I want to go in Europe, and how long did I want to spend at each stop? I had a month booked off work and was hungry to see all of Europe. Off to the local book shop I went in search of the book *Europe Through the Back Door*. I picked it up as well as a couple of other guidebooks about Italy, France, and Greece.

For the next several months, Greg and I read the books and dog-eared pages we liked, searched online, and continued to watch Rick Steves. Every night, our conversations revolved around our upcoming trip, trying to decide whether to book accommodation or just show up. We finally settled on an itinerary.

After several long and impatient months, the time for our trip had arrived! We flew from Vancouver, Canada, to Heathrow Airport in London. This was going to be the first stop of an adventure that was completely outside my comfort zone.

We had accommodation for three nights in London with friends of friends (strangers to me). At this point in time, I was a fairly timid traveler—always pre-booking chain hotels, booking transportation ahead of time, and generally staying within my known experiences, so staying with strangers was a bit unnerving.

Following Rick Steves' Advice

After landing at the airport and taking the Underground into the center of London, we hitched our backpacks and walked several blocks to the address we had been given. Rob and Angie met us at the door with a big hello and a cocktail. They ended up being the most amazing hosts.

During the three days we spent with them, they took us to the local hotspots to drink beers and watch the local sports teams, gave us directions to sites we wanted to see, and provided tips for other unusual things to do and see. We drank in pubs with the locals, hit the major night clubs until 5 am, shopped in Harrods, and ate some of the best Indian food I had ever had at that point in time. It was a great start to the trip.

Next up was Paris, which has been on my bucket list since I was a little girl. Because neither Greg nor I speak French, we pre-booked our hotel in the Latin Quarter as we didn't want to waste time searching for accommodation.

When I was booking our trip, I had to figure out how to get from England to France. Would we take the ferry? The Chunnel? Or fly? I carefully researched each option and easily decided that we would fly, especially since I found the best flight deal I had ever seen.

Sites and Bites

BMI Airlines was offering a flight from London to Paris for £7.50, with a £2.50 discount for paying immediately. That was shocking. To convert that, this equaled $10 Canadian dollars. Not quite believing this to be true, I booked two flights. When Greg and I showed up at the airport, I expected to be told that there wasn't a flight. Surprise, surprise, there was actually a flight. We checked our bags and boarded the plane.

Another surprise awaited. The seats were soft leather with lots of arm and legroom. We were given a choice of three newspapers and three magazines to read (and take with us). Then, we were served a gin & tonic (my drink of choice) and given a couple of shortbread cookies. The hour and twenty-minute flight passed beautifully, with a second cocktail being served. Since this flight, I've taken a lot of flights, but I've never been treated as special as I was on BMI.

Arriving at Charles De Gaulle airport, we collected our luggage, caught the train into the city centre and made our way to our hotel. We were tired from the late nights in London and the jet lag, so we made it an early night.

The following morning, I was up first. I couldn't believe it, I was actually in Paris! I took a quick shower and decided to let Greg sleep while I went in search of coffee and a croissant.

Following Rick Steves' Advice

I walked into the coffee shop beside the hotel and attempted to order two coffees and two croissants to go. I said bonjour and placed my order. Paying at the counter, I waited for my order. The server placed my plated croissants and china-cup served coffees on the counter. I was surprised to see this. Was I allowed to take the dishes out of the restaurant to the hotel? I flagged down the server and tried to explain that I wanted to have a take-away order. The man eventually understood me and proceeded to yell at me in French for several moments before snatching away my order and stomping away.

Since I had no idea what he actually said to me, I stood there, not knowing what to do. Was he coming back? Was I supposed to leave? I was frozen with indecision. After what felt like hours but was probably just a few minutes, my server came back to the counter with my coffees in to-go cups and slammed them down before stomping off.

I smiled, said merci, and left with coffee and croissants for breakfast. I even had a huge smile on my face. I am a shy person, and being yelled at in public normally would have left me mortified, but I survived the encounter and didn't die from embarrassment. At that moment, my confidence grew, and I knew that I would be able to manage traveling in a country that spoke a different language than I knew.

Sites and Bites

The rest of my time in Paris was amazing. I sat in several sidewalk cafés drinking wine and spending time people-watching. I visited several well-known museums, walked the streets and window shopped, took in the Eiffel Tower, and ate the most delicious food. Taking Rick Steves' advice, we ordered the prix fix menu when eating out for dinner and weren't disappointed. Four days later, we rented a car and moved on to other parts of Europe.

There were three weeks left of our trip, and we had no accommodation booked for any of it, a very uncomfortable situation for me. But our intention was to find quaint places to stay by interacting with the locals. Not as easy as it sounds.

Driving south, we headed for the beaches. Our destination was Saint-Tropez. Driving in France was harder than I thought. Our car didn't have GPS, and all we had was a paper map and a general idea of where we were going. The highways were faster than we were used to in Canada, and all of the signs, of course, were in French.

Needless to say, after seven hours of driving and having no idea where we were, Greg and I were very cranky and snapping at each other. Greg pulled off the highway, and we ended up at a place called La Ciotat. Deciding we needed to call it a day, Greg parked the car, and we

Following Rick Steves' Advice

booked a night at the first hotel we came to. We grabbed a bite to eat in the closest restaurant and took a walk on the windswept beach before turning in.

The next day was sunny, and we were both in a better mood. We continued on our way to Saint-Tropez but ended up stopping for lunch in Saint-Raphaël, never realizing that we had bypassed our destination. Saint-Raphaël's beach was stunning, and we decided to spend some time sunning ourselves. By late afternoon, neither Greg nor I wanted to leave, so we found a small hotel half a block from the beach.

Using my newfound confidence, I booked a room with a private bath using a combination of broken French (me) and broken English (hotel staff) with the friendly desk clerk. We stayed a week in Saint-Raphaël and spent time walking around town, sunbathing, and being served food and drink on the beach by beautiful people. Eventually, we moved on and headed to Italy without ever seeing Saint-Tropez. I guess that will have to be for the next trip.

We dropped off our car in Saint-Raphaël and took the train to Italy. First stop: Florence, where we were able to rent a second car. Off we drove into the hills of Italy. We were looking for an Agriturismo, an independently owned farm with available accommodation, so it made sense to check out the Tourism Centre in Greve for some help. We headed there only to find they were closed for lunch, but the sign said they would be open at 2 pm. With nothing else to do, Greg and I walked around the town and waited. At 2 pm, we headed back to the tourist centre, but it wasn't open yet, so we continued to wait. 3 pm, still not open. At 4 pm, we realized that it was probably not going to open at all, so we had a decision to make about where we would stay that night.

How hard could it be to find our own accommodation? With Greg driving and me on the lookout for Turismo signs, we drove through the Tuscan countryside searching for vacancy signs with no success. After a couple of hours with no luck and starting to feel frustrated, we came across the gates to a vineyard with a small sign and entered. Thankfully, the people who owned the gorgeous 800-year-old farmhouse had a room available and we booked ourselves in for four days.

Close to the farmhouse was a monastery that brewed its own beer, and we walked the dirt road to partake a couple of times during our stay. Our accommodation had a pool for relaxing beside, and the family who owned the farm invited us to have lunch with them. Lunch included homemade bread, sausage, pate, marinated vegetables and

Following Rick Steves' Advice

wine. Lots and lots of wine from their cellar. No wonder siestas last from 2 pm to 5 pm!

Evenings found Greg and I visiting the nearby hilltop towns for dinner, which didn't start until 8 pm. Definitely not the norm for this Canadian! Starting at 8 pm and being served multiple courses, dinner didn't finish until 10 pm or later. Then, it was time to sit in the square with the locals, eating the best gelato ever and drinking coffee.

After four days in this beautiful area of Italy, we decided to head to Greece, another bucket list destination for me. We dropped off our car in Florence and caught the high-speed train to Rome, where, with the help of our Turismo hosts, we had booked a small B&B for one night.

Arriving at Rome's train station, I grabbed my luggage and stepped outside so we could catch a taxi to our place. I was overwhelmed by the helpful drivers clamoring for our business. One taxi driver approached, grabbed my luggage, felt my ass, threw my bag into the trunk of his cab, and hopped into the driver's seat. I stood there stunned; it had happened so quickly. My husband was already in the taxi, so I got in, and we arrived at our accommodation within a couple of minutes. I let my husband pay; there was no way I was getting anywhere close to the driver.

Sites and Bites

As our taxi sped away, Greg looked at me and asked, "What's up? You seem distracted." I explained what had happened with the driver, and then we both stood there, sort of stunned and at a loss for what to do. Then, as we looked at each other, we started to laugh. There really was nothing we could do at that point. It became our joke over the rest of our trip: my friendly introduction to Rome.

We spent one busy day in Rome, walking everywhere. We visited the Colosseum, and while we were there, we were approached by a man wearing a gladiator suit. He asked if we wanted to take our picture with him. Of course, we said yes. After the pictures were taken, he told us we had to pay him 20 euros. In hindsight, I guess we could have walked away from him, but we handed over the cash.

Throughout the day, we came across many ruins, fountains, and crazy traffic. It was so fun. That evening, we ate dinner on a restaurant patio beside a huge water fountain, and then, later, we followed a crowd of people to a hilltop to watch the sunset over Rome. It's a city that I must return to.

The following morning, we caught a bus to the airport for our flight to Athens. I've never been so scared in my life. Our bus driver seemed to have a death wish, driving 120 miles per hour in massive amounts of traffic, tailgating

Following Rick Steves' Advice

everyone, and changing lanes with no regard for other drivers. It was so scary that I almost kissed the ground when we arrived safely at the airport.

We flew from Rome to Athens, then caught the ferry to Santorini. To say that the ferry ride was different from the ferries in Canada would be an understatement. Our eight-hour trip had us sunbathing on the loungers, drinking Heineken with strangers, and even having shots of Ouzo with a Greek family celebrating a birthday. I was already in love with Greece!

We spent a week here, two days on the cliffside of the island, and the rest of the time sunbathing, hiking, and drinking on the beachside. It was the perfect last week of our trip.

At the end of the week, we retraced our steps with a late ferry ride back to Athens and a midnight bus ride to the airport. There was no reason to get a hotel room as our flight from Athens to London was scheduled to leave at 6 am.

Around 4 am, Greg and I were close to our check-in counter, waiting for the staff to arrive. At 5 am, we noticed that other airlines' check-in counters were starting to open, but not ours. Feeling some panic as our flight to

Sites and Bites

London was connecting to our return to Vancouver, we politely asked at two counters to see if we could get help with our flight.

One staff member from a different airline spent a lot of time searching for answers for us only to eventually let us know that apparently our flight had been cancelled and no ticket agent for our airline was going to show up because there was no flight! Scrambling now to book a flight that would see us arrive in London for our connection home, we ended up flying to Amsterdam, then on to London and finally back to Vancouver.

Now, I'm not sure if this trip is what Rick Steves meant when he said to connect with the locals, but despite the unexpected and unusual things that happened, I can honestly say this was the best trip, and it was what sparked my current travel lust.

CHAPTER 2

Taj Mahal Tourist Attraction

I was quite fascinated with all things India; I watched every food special, travel show, and nature documentary that had anything at all to do with the country. I couldn't explain it. I don't particularly like Indian food (I'm not a fan of curry, and I don't eat rice). The tales of the poisonous snakes freaked me out, and I was disgusted by how polluted the Ganges River was. But still, I couldn't stop watching shows about it. This went on for a couple of years.

Then came the year my son and husband got me a very special birthday present. As my son stated, "Mom, I know we're not very patient when you want to stop and take photos, so we're sending you on a photo trip by yourself." I was in shock. What a great gift!

My husband said they hadn't purchased the trip yet because they weren't sure which trip I preferred. They had options for Iceland and Croatia, both of which were on my list of places to visit. I thanked them with big hugs and said, "I want to go to India!"

I think they were both surprised. They knew I wasn't a fan of the food and thought I wanted to take landscape photos. I did, but I felt a real drive to get to India.

I did some research to find a photography trip, but all the well-known brands were super expensive. I was beginning to despair that I would never go. Then, one day at lunch, while reading the paper, I saw an advertisement for a photo trip to India that was affordable and included airfare.

Before I could change my mind, I called the number and booked and paid for my trip. I was going to India! I texted my son and husband, told them the dates, and then ordered a celebratory cocktail.

Over the next few months, I had to get ready for the trip. I had to apply for a visa and get all the vaccinations needed,

Taj Mahal Tourist Attraction

and there were a lot. I think I'm safe to go anywhere now. I carefully read all the instructions for travel, packing, and money, while also ensuring that both of my cameras were ready to go.

Finally, the day arrived, and I was off to the airport. After a long, chaotic flight, the plane landed in New Delhi. I grabbed my carry-on luggage and joined the long line for customs and immigration. After being fingerprinted and photographed at security, I stepped outside into the heat to meet the tour guide and the others on the tour. There were 12 people on this tour, and I was ready to get to know all of them in the next two weeks.

The great thing about the tour was that the accommodations were beautiful, no worries about poor or unsafe locations. For the next four days, the group was taken out to explore. I quickly realized that the tour wasn't going to meet my expectations of a photo tour. Yes, we were at locations where it was beautiful enough to take a lot of pictures, but there was no attempt to get out early or late to capture the light. This tour seemed to be more about visiting tourist sites and shopping from local vendors, not at all what I signed up for.

Then came the Taj Mahal. It had been a long travel day and we went directly to our hotel for the night. After check-in, the tour group met in the restaurant for dinner and to get instructions from our guide. He advised that the entrance rules to the Taj Mahal were very strict and that if we didn't abide by them, the group wouldn't be allowed onto the grounds.

Taj Mahal entrance rules:

- No food or drink
- No gum
- No labels on clothing
- No flags, pins, or anything that showed your country
- No religious symbols of any kind
- No weapons

The morning of our visit, we all met in the lobby at 4:30 am to ensure that we had lots of time to get inside the gates and watch the sunrise. It was a short bus ride from our hotel to the gates of the Taj Mahal. I had envisioned it being fairly quiet since it was dark and only 5 am. What a shock! The tour bus pulled up beside several other buses, an abundance of cars, and people. The area was packed!

Getting into the Taj Mahal grounds wasn't quick. First, the men and women get separated; each sex has its own gate and lineup. The next step is to show your ID and

Taj Mahal Tourist Attraction

get searched. After the search and the ID verification process, there's another lineup. I was instructed to place my camera bag on the side so it could go through the X-ray machine, and then the bag was searched. Finally, I had to step through a scanner before picking up my bag. But I was through!

Due to the massive amounts of people and the thorough security, I would say it took close to 45 minutes before I was allowed onto the grounds. My tour guide gathered us all up, and we went to get a look at the famous building. It was simply incredible.

Shuffling past thousands of other people, our guide was trying to gather the group so we could pose for a picture in front of the Taj Mahal, for sale, of course, if we wanted copies. I was getting very annoyed. This wasn't what I signed up for. I noticed that two of the other women on the tour were creeping away; they also wanted to take their own photographs, so I decided to do the same.

Keeping an eye on my tour group, I went about photographing the temple. But there were so many people that getting a photo without hundreds of others in it was impossible. Just as I was getting used to the idea that I wasn't going to get the perfect photo, a very old Indian man approached. He had a proposal for me. For

20 Canadian dollars, he would give me a tour and help me get the photos I was after. It sounded like a great deal for me, so I agreed. I tried to pay him, but he refused, stating he would collect his money after the tour.

For the next hour, I followed him around the grounds while he cleared people away from my shot. There was no way I would have managed without this man. After paying him his well-deserved $20, I went to look for my group. By this time, the sun was up, and the grounds were packed. It felt like there were a hundred thousand people. I spent the next 30 minutes looking for my group before I realized this was a lost cause. I decided to sit on the steps where we entered. That way, they would have to come past me.

Sitting there was such an enjoyable experience. I had a beautiful view of the Taj Mahal; there were so many people coming and going that it was great for people-watching, and the sun was out—a perfect morning. I'm not sure how long I sat there watching people sitting, standing, taking photos and selfies before I became aware of something very odd.

People were taking selfies with me in them! Once I became aware of it, I noticed it happening over and over again. Some people were trying to be discreet about it,

Taj Mahal Tourist Attraction

sitting on a lower step and catching me in their shot; others were sitting right beside me for a quick shot before jumping up and going away.

I can't tell you how I felt. At first, I was amused, then annoyed, then puzzled. Why would all these people want a selfie with me in it? It continued to happen for the entire hour that I sat there waiting for my tour group. Eventually, my group walked past me, and I joined them, heading back to the bus.

After we were all back on the bus and driving back to the hotel, I told my guide what had happened, and he started laughing. Eventually, he explained that I was an oddity in his country because of my looks. That made sense; with my pale skin, blond hair, and blue eyes, I definitely wasn't the norm in India.

When I visited the Taj Mahal, it seemed like hundreds of people had taken my photo. I suspect it's now all over Instagram, and that's the day I became a tourist attraction!

CHAPTER 3

Scary Plane Ride

Since I had booked a photography tour to India, I didn't have control of the flight itinerary, which is why I ended up flying from Vancouver to New Delhi via Toronto.

The flight from Vancouver to Toronto was just your typical flight: show up a couple of hours early, get through security with my carry-on luggage, and wait. I was pretty excited, so the wait seemed forever, but finally, the airport staff loaded the plane, and off we went. Flying from Vancouver to Toronto is a flight I have taken several times, and I passed the five hours reading and napping.

Upon arrival at Pearson Airport, I found the gate where my next flight would be and went to hang around. I don't find airports to be that interesting, so I found a chair and a glass of wine and read my book for the next three hours. At some point, close to boarding time, I realized the area of the airport where I sat was packed. I've never seen so many people in one spot outside of a festival.

I grabbed my luggage and went to my gate to wait for the boarding call. When the airline staff show up at the gate, the crowd of passengers always seems to get excited. Yippee, we're boarding! That was the case here. The flight attendant announced they would be boarding the plane by section and to please remain seated until your section was called.

The entire crowd of passengers stood up and pushed forward. The flight attendant announced again that everyone should remain seated as they were boarding people who needed extra help. The crowd never sat down. I was standing close to my boarding lane and continued to stand and wait patiently.

As soon as the flight attendant processed a lady in a wheelchair and what appeared to be her husband, the crowd of passengers leaned forward.

Scary Plane Ride

"Please wait for your section to be called," said the airline staff member.

The crowd backed up slightly. She processed another person who clearly needed some extra time to board, and the crowd pushed forward again.

"Get back," she said into her microphone.

The crowd backed up again. By this point, I was starting to feel nervous. There was tension in the air, and I was surrounded by hundreds of people who seemed to be on the verge of something. I grabbed my bag and pushed out of the crowd to stand across the concourse. I'm used to a fairly organized and patient boarding, so this was very strange to me. A second flight attendant showed up, and the crowd leaned forward again.

"Please back up and wait for your section to be called," he announced. The two attendants started to process the first section for boarding, and suddenly, hundreds of people were trying to get through the checkpoint first.

"Please, back up!" came the shout. This time, the crowd didn't back up.

Sites and Bites

Across the way, I stood there watching in disbelief. The plane wouldn't take off without its passengers, so I didn't understand why everyone was surging forward. I saw the female flight attendant pick up the phone, not sure who she was calling, while the male attendant kept yelling for people to get back. No one was listening. The crowd of passengers was moving forward, waving their passports in the air, trying to get through the checkpoint.

Soon, two security guards showed up, trying to control the crowd. It quickly became apparent they weren't having any success. From my vantage point, it was hard to see the staff at the counter, but finally, I did, as security pushed them away from the crowd. It suddenly became a free-for-all!

Hundreds of people began pushing themselves through the door and down the ramp to the plane, pushing and shoving each other as they went. Eventually, most of the passengers cleared, and I decided that now was a good time for me to board. The flight attendants and security people were nowhere to be found, so I just followed where the crowd went without anyone checking my passport.

I assumed that the craziness was over, but I was wrong. The onboard attendants were trying to direct people and

Scary Plane Ride

be helpful about seating, but it was like they weren't being heard. People were still shoving each other.

The plane was probably one of the biggest ones I've ever been on. There were three seats on each of the window sides and rows of six across in the middle, making it awkward to get to your seat if you went down the wrong aisle. The plane was huge, and the flight appeared to be full. I managed to find my aisle seat and placed my carry-on luggage above my head before sitting down. Thankfully, the row I was in was completely full already, so I didn't have to worry about standing up to let anyone in.

As I settled in for the 15-hour flight, I was fascinated by the other passengers. While most passengers seemed to be seated, there were still too many to count who were standing and yelling at each other. One woman was in the aisle, yelling at a man in his seat. To me, it looked like he was refusing to stand and let her get to her seat. She continued to yell for a minute before jumping on him and trying to climb into her seat. As he started yelling and pushing her, the crew rushed over to stop what was happening.

Off to my right, another kerfuffle was happening. Two men were yelling at each other in a language I didn't understand. One of the men turned his back to the second

Sites and Bites

man and then put his luggage in the overhead bin. The second man reached over, pulled out the luggage, dropped it to the floor, and then put his luggage in the bin. The first man picked up his luggage, grabbed the other guy's luggage and threw it across the plane, hitting another passenger about five rows away. That man got up and started yelling. I don't know what was said, but suddenly the man who the bag had hit was climbing across the tops of the rows and people trying to get to the men in the original argument. Again, the flight crew intervened.

Just as the luggage argument quieted down, another started in the row in front of me. It turns out that two people had the exact same name and were issued a ticket for the exact same seat. I'm sure that would've been caught earlier at the boarding gate if the crowd hadn't pushed past the staff without any passport check.

The two fellows were escorted from the plane to sort it out while we all waited. The flight was now 40 minutes late from the scheduled departure time. When the men came back with the seats sorted out, I thought, finally, we can go. But I was wrong again.

Two women in the same row but at opposite ends stood up, screaming at each other and throwing things: magazines, pamphlets, clothes, whatever they could get their hands

Scary Plane Ride

on. Two flight attendants rushed over to settle that down. The pilot finally got on the PA system and announced they wouldn't move and would stay on the runway all night unless everyone settled down immediately. Thankfully, they did.

The 15-hour flight went smoothly after that until the plane touched down. Long before the plane stopped moving, the majority of the passengers were up, grabbing their luggage, and trying to either push past people or climb over seats to get to the exit door. I wisely stayed put until the plane was mostly empty. When I finally disembarked, I thought that was the craziest plane ride I had ever experienced.

After two fabulous weeks in India, I was back at the airport in Delhi, waiting for a direct flight to Vancouver. I was very glad it was direct, as I was still in disbelief at the Toronto flight.

The security at the Indira Gandhi International Airport was heavy, including armed guards everywhere. Along with regular security checks when you arrive at the airport, there are extra metal detectors at each boarding gate and baggage checks where all your belongings are looked at. There was no way that anyone could get on this flight without a passport check.

Sites and Bites

The return flight was once again on a large plane with a full passenger list. Loading went smoothly, and I was glad to begin my journey home. For the return flight, I managed to get an emergency exit seat with lots of legroom.

During takeoff, a flight attendant sat in her seat facing me; I was close enough to hear her on the phone to the pilot stating that we were good in the cabin.

After a smooth takeoff, the cabin staff started to bring out the food and drink trolleys; we had been in the air for about 15 minutes at that point. Suddenly, a woman a few rows ahead of me and to my right started screaming. Two flight attendants rushed over to see what was happening. I couldn't see what was happening with the woman from my seat, but one of the attendants rushed back to the phone in front of me and paged the cabin, "Is there a doctor on board?" I was suddenly sick to my stomach. With all the times that I have flown, it has never occurred to me that there might be a need for a doctor.

One of the passengers got up and went to help; the woman was still screaming in pain. Suddenly, behind me, a man started yelling for help. Since the screaming woman seemed to be getting help, the flight attendants rushed back to the man. His friend had suddenly passed out, and he couldn't

Scary Plane Ride

get him to wake up. The flight attendant rushed back to her seat and picked up the phone. I'm not sure who she was speaking to, but she was explaining what was happening in the cabin; they had no doctor on board and needed help. She was speaking with the other person and then started saying, "Well, we could touch down in Pakistan."

Pakistan? What? At first, I thought, *well, won't that be a story to tell my friends at home?* Then I started to think, *wait a minute. I don't have a visa for this country; what if they detain us or throw us in jail? No one would know where I am.* I was starting to panic. The crew member noticed my expression, said something quietly into the phone, hung up, and walked away.

Suddenly, the online flight maps located on the seat backs went dark, and I could no longer see where we were flying. I was racking my brain, trying to figure out how to contact my family back home to let them know what was happening. I left Canada for two weeks in India without my cell phone and now wished I had it. We flew for another 15 minutes when the woman stopped screaming, and when I stood up to look, she appeared to be sleeping. At least, that was what I hoped she was doing. The man behind me seemed okay; he was awake and talking to his seatmate. As we flew on, the airplane seemed extra quiet to me.

Eventually, the steward staff brought out the food and drink carts and loaded everyone up with all the food and drink they wanted. I think they were trying to keep us all busy. When we eventually landed in Vancouver, without an emergency landing in Pakistan, I waited to see if medics were going to board to address the woman who had been screaming. But no one boarded, and she stood up on her own and disembarked.

When I finally got off the plane and through customs, I was extremely happy to see my husband and son there to pick me up. On the way home, I entertained them with the story of my crazy flights.

CHAPTER 4

Where Are My Socks?

I know a lot of people who like to pack for their vacation several days prior to their trip. They all claim that it helps them be ready and lessens the stress of travel. I have never agreed with that philosophy, though I have tried to be that organized. However, it always leaves with me the thought that I've forgotten to pack something, and then I continue to check and recheck my luggage prior to my trip. So now, I usually pack just a few hours before I'm ready to start my journey.

This was the case the night my friend Rosh came over for a pre-vacation cocktail. Her parents were in town for a visit, and she was introducing them to everyone she knew. Since it was a beautiful summer evening, it seemed appropriate to sit in the backyard to enjoy a glass of wine and chat.

My husband opened the wine, and I took out the glasses. Soon, we were engaged in conversations about South Africa, Toronto, and traveling in general. I found Rosh's parents, Vino and Lutchmee, to be quite entertaining. As the night wore on, more bottles of wine were opened, and the laughter never stopped. Both Lutchmee and Vino were so funny.

As the evening got later, I grabbed a couple of blankets for everyone to ward against the chill of the evening, and Greg brought out a speaker and turned on some music. Rosh said they were leaving a few times, but then another glass of wine was poured, and no one went anywhere. Eventually, the conversation slowed enough that everyone thought it was best to call it a night. To my shock, I noticed that it was 3 am. I had an 8 am flight and hadn't even packed yet.

With a flurry of activity, Greg and I hustled Rosh and her parents into a taxi and cleaned up as best as we could. We had both consumed quite a bit of wine and were not functioning clearly. Knowing that we still had to pack

Where Are My Socks?

but weren't quite able to do so, we decided to have a quick nap before packing. We set the alarm and passed out.

Of course, we missed the alarm, but thankfully, I woke up before our flight was supposed to leave. In a panic, I woke Greg up, jumped into the shower, called a cab, and started to throw clothes into my suitcase. By the time the taxi came 15 minutes later, we were both packed and ready to go. Greg and I were still tipsy, but somehow, we made our flight in time.

We were flying to Winnipeg to stay with Greg's dad, Bob, for the long weekend. At this point, I had only met Bob once. I slept the entire three-hour flight, and I'm sure Greg did too. Bob was there at the airport to pick us up. When we arrived at his home, Greg informed him that we had a late night and needed to nap. I was embarrassed since we had just arrived, but I was unable to function well at this point. We both crawled into bed and napped for a couple of hours.

Getting up, I decided to take a shower to freshen up. As I was getting dressed afterward, I realized I didn't have any socks. In my panic earlier in the day, I didn't pack them. When Greg got out of his shower, I told him my issue, only for him to laugh and say he had forgotten to pack his underwear.

Into the living room we went to ask Bob if he could drive up to the closest Shoppers Drug Mart as we had forgotten socks and underwear. I was mortified that on my second introduction to my father-in-law, I needed him to help me shop. Bob was gracious about it and drove us to the shop, waiting in the car while Greg and I ran in and made our purchase.

The rest of the afternoon was wonderful—visiting with Bob, listening to his funny stories about where he worked, and just hanging around the backyard. We had a nice BBQ for dinner and just hung out. What started out as a frantic day had ended up being fabulous until bedtime.

Getting ready for bed, I changed into my pajamas and went to wash my face and brush my teeth, only to be horrified. Not only had I forgotten my socks, but I also didn't pack my toothbrush. I definitely couldn't go three days without brushing my teeth. I felt like crying. I was sure that Bob was going to judge me poorly. Just then, Greg walked into the bathroom and said, "I forgot my toothpaste." I started laughing. What a couple of goofs we turned out to be.

Greg went to his dad and told him that we had to return to the store as we had more items we needed to replace. Thankfully, Bob just laughed as he asked, "Did you guys pack anything for this trip?" before driving us back to the store to pick up the essentials. While picking up a new toothbrush, I also bought body lotion, deodorant, sunscreen, and bug spray (essential in Winnipeg). I wasn't taking any chances that I had forgotten anything else. The rest of our weekend was fabulous; the only shopping that we needed to do was for groceries and wine.

I'm sure there's a lesson here, but is the lesson pack before your trip? Or don't party before you pack? Either way, I'm not sure I've learned it.

CHAPTER 5

Wedding Crasher in Vancouver

When I lived in Vancouver, I made a lot of good friends, so when I moved out of the city, I kept in touch with them all. One weekend, a girls' night out was planned, and since I lived close by, I was able to make the event.

Looking forward to the night, I arrived in the city early and made my way to the meet-up location. We were all meeting at a bar on Hastings Street. I was a bit nervous as sections of Hastings Street have a sketchy reputation, and I didn't want to wait out on the street, so I entered the bar about 30 minutes before the expected time.

Sites and Bites

The only person in the bar was the bartender, and instead of sitting at one of the empty tables, I chose to sit at the end of the bar to wait. The bartender served me a glass of white wine, and I opened my phone to scroll through social media.

Keeping one eye on the time, I ordered a second glass of wine and continued to wait for my friends to show up. As I waited, I randomly surfed the web. I was almost finished with my second glass of wine when I noticed the time. My friends were about 20 minutes late. I was somewhat annoyed, but since the bar was filling up, I had a chance to people-watch.

There was a real excitement to the crowd; a lot of drinks were being ordered, the music was loud, and people were laughing. At some point, a woman wandered over to where I was sitting. There was a water station, and she was getting a glass of it for herself. She introduced herself as Kathy and said she was from Williams Lake. She asked if I lived locally or up north (Northern BC). I told her I was a local, and she said, "That's why I haven't seen you before," before she wandered away with her water.

I was thinking that was a very weird interaction when another woman came over to get some water. The bar was packed full of people at this point and was getting very warm. This woman, Shannon, started talking to me like I should know a lot of people in the room, telling me she was very happy for the bride and groom, even though she dated the groom first. She told me about her small children and her job, which she had taken time off from to come to Vancouver this weekend. Just as Shannon was about to return to her table, another woman came over and started talking. Before I knew it, the three of us were discussing children, babysitting concerns, and what it was like to date when you had children.

As they walked away from me, I looked at my watch and realized my friends were over an hour late. I was starting to get cranky. I hate waiting for long periods of time, but I didn't have any other plans, so I ordered another glass of wine and waited for the next person to pop over for water. Realizing that the crowd was all friends, I thought I could just sit quietly at the end of the bar. However, more and more people kept coming over for water. At one point, I was asked who I knew at the party, and happily, I was able to point out Kathy and Shannon and provide some personal details about them. This seemed to satisfy my questioner.

During a quiet time by the water cooler, I checked my phone for any messages from my friends and found they were all texting me. The text messages said that they couldn't get into the bar. It was a private event. I didn't understand what they were talking about. When I arrived, there was no private event sign nor a doorman, and I texted them that. They kept insisting that the doorman wouldn't let them in due to the private party.

Resigned to leaving, I was going to finish my wine, pay my bill, and go to where my friends were. But before I could finish my wine, my friend Katherine sat down beside me. She explained that she begged her way past the doorman in order to get me. Since she was there, it felt appropriate that she order a glass of wine while I finished mine.

As we sat there, people kept coming for water, including my new friend Shannon. Katherine and I chatted with everyone, gathering information without giving away the fact that we weren't invited to the party. We were giggling and having so much fun that Katherine and I ordered more wine, rudely ignoring the fact that our other friends were still outside the bar with no way in.

And as I knew it must happen, a man finally sat beside us and said, "You guys don't know anyone here, do you?"

With a quick look at each other, Katherine and I admitted we didn't and explained about meeting our friends here.

Wedding Crasher in Vancouver

He laughed hard, introduced himself as Dave and said he would keep our secret for us. It turns out that Dave was the Best Man at the wedding, and Katherine and I had crashed a wedding reception without even knowing it. He then introduced us to more people, and before you knew it, Katherine and I were doing shots with the groomsmen.

We spent the next couple of hours drinking wine, engaging in conversations with strangers, and dancing with the groom and the groom's father. The usual party photos were taken, and I even have some of Katherine with the groom on my phone. Eventually, I noticed that the crowd was starting to thin out.

Not wanting to be noticed by the bride, I paid our bar tab and Katherine and I left the bar, our friends long gone for the night. It was one of the most fun wedding receptions I had ever been to, and I didn't even have an invite.

I often wonder if Katherine and I made it into the wedding photo book that most brides print. And if so, would Dave still be keeping our secret, and would people still be trying to figure out who the two women drinking shots with the wedding party members were?

CHAPTER 6

Family Christmas in Manzanillo

Wanting to get away from the stress and commercialism of the Christmas season, my husband and I decided that we would try an all-inclusive holiday in Mexico. I spent some time researching a resort that was appropriate for our eight-year-old son, my husband and I, and my mother-in-law, Gail, who was joining us.

I found a great deal at a small resort in Manzanillo, Mexico, where our room was called a junior suite. The suite was open plan with two queen beds and a large living room. The balcony overlooked the main pool and palm trees and had a peek-a-boo ocean view. The

600-square-foot suite would be home to the four of us for the next two weeks.

We arrived at the resort on December 23, ready to relax and have some fun. The check-in process went smoothly, and we took our luggage to our room. My son, Denby, shared the bed with Grandma and my husband and I had the bed closest to the living room and balcony.

The next three days were magical. The sun shone all day, the temperature was perfect for the beach and for playing in the sand, Christmas music was playing, the hundreds of poinsettias were the largest I had ever seen, a giant Christmas tree was in the lobby, and food was everywhere. On Christmas morning, Santa drove in from the beach on his golf cart to hand out gifts to the children.

For three days, we ate, drank mimosas and Chi Chi cocktails on the beach, built sandcastles, and swam. On days four and five, I noticed that Gail and my husband were using the bathroom a lot. Montezuma's Revenge? I have a don't ask, don't tell policy about that.

Our resort was perfect, but sometimes it felt small, so we started to take trips offsite as a family. We walked along the beach, went to offsite restaurants, and took a trip into the center of Manzanillo. Unfortunately, the

Family Christmas in Manzanillo

day we were going into town, Gail was with us briefly before she had to head back to the resort. She wanted to stay close to the bathroom. Greg, Denby, and I spent the afternoon walking around town before heading back to the resort. Poor Grandma spent the day inside the suite and close to the toilet.

By the end of the first week, the flaws of having four people in one room, even a nice-sized one, were starting to show. Gail was a big snorer. And loud. Wow. One night was so bad that Greg sat up in bed and slammed a pillow on top of her head to stop the snoring. All she did was roll over and continue to snore. Another night, Greg was so cranky due to the loud snoring that I left the bed and slept in the balcony chair. Not a lounger, a chair.

The resort had a nice, protected beach, and it was perfect for snorkelling or swimming with a small child, but from time to time, Greg wanted the waves. There was a gated exit along the sand, and we often used it for morning walks or to frequent the local restaurants. The security guard would check our resort passes before letting us in. Very secure.

One day, we left the resort a bit later than normal and headed to our favourite beachside restaurant. We filled up on seafood and margaritas (Denby's had no alcohol) and watched the sun go down. Beautiful. After dinner, we walked along the beach in the dark back to our resort. After a 45-minute walk, we found a couple of changes. First, the tide had come in, and a small section of the beach was now underwater. We would have to cross that in order to get to the gate. Hoping that there weren't any dangerous fish in the water, Greg hoisted Denby on his shoulders, and we all crossed the water, getting soaked up to our knees. The second difference? The gate was no longer manned by a security guard and was, in fact, locked. We were unable to open it or scale it.

Back along the moonlit beach we went to find that the restaurant was now closed, and we had to find a taxi to take us back to the resort. Four tourists, three semi-drunk and one a child, walking the streets in the dark in an unfamiliar place didn't feel very safe to me. Eventually, we found a taxi, but no one could communicate with the driver as he only spoke Spanish, and we only spoke English. As we were sitting in the taxi, feeling frustrated, this little voice spoke up. The next thing I knew, Denby spoke enough Spanish for the driver to understand where we needed to go. When we arrived at the resort, Denby figured out the money for the ride. It was somewhat embarrassing that my eight-year-old was the one who

Family Christmas in Manzanillo

managed to get us back home, but at the same time, impressive.

At this point in the trip, Gail was spending a couple of hours a day at the adult-only pool, just relaxing. But one afternoon, we were headed to the beach outside the resort to play in the waves, and Gail wanted to join us. As we exited the side gate, I asked the security guard what time they would be locking up; I wasn't going to get locked out again!

The section of the beach where we stopped had some big, six-foot waves, and we raced along the sand, trying to see how close we could come to the water's edge before the next wave hit. It was a lot of fun. Suddenly, the waves became bigger, and we all got wet. The worst part was how much the waves were sucking at us to pull us back into the ocean. I don't know how to swim, and I was worried about Denby getting sucked out to sea. I looked back at Denby, and he was hanging on to Greg and squealing with laughter.

Gail and I were closer to dry land but still getting hit by the waves, and as I stood in place, with the water rushing out to sea, the sand below my feet changed. Wave by wave, I was getting sucked into the sand. I yelled over to Gail to tell her about my feet in the sand when a big wave hit her.

Sites and Bites

The wave took her down and pushed her farther up the sand. But then, when the water rushed back, it dragged her out to sea. Another wave hit her, and she rolled up the beach only to be sucked back down. Over and over again she rolled, her arms like windmills as the waves rolled her back and forth.

Gail was screaming, "Help me!" but I was laughing so hard that I couldn't help and I was struggling to stay upright myself in the waves. I could hear Denby yelling in encouragement, "Get up, Grandma!" but Gail kept rolling up and down the beach. At some point, the waves washed her far enough up the beach that the receding water didn't suck her back.

Greg and Denby managed to make their way to where she was, but I was still struggling to get away from the water. Finally, the four of us were on dry land together. Gail looked like a drowned rat. I asked her if she was ok, to which she responded, "I don't know if I have sand in my pants or if I shit myself." Denby laughed so hard at that answer. Gail decided she had enough of the beach and went back to the resort. Greg, Denby, and I stayed a while longer.

Later that night at dinner, Denby asked Gail, "Grandma, was it sand in your pants?" Gail responded, "It was a bit

Family Christmas in Manzanillo

of both," and we all laughed. That was the last day during our vacation that Grandma joined us on the beach, and she spent the rest of the trip at the adult-only pool with a good book.

CHAPTER 7

Cinque Terre Sleepover

My husband and I were visiting Italy, and we stayed in Rome for two nights before moving on. Our goal was to see several parts of Italy. We had no specific plans and no hotels booked. The morning of our third day found us at Rome's main train station, ready to go. You can reach the Cinque Terre from Rome in a few hours by taking the high-speed train to La Spezia and then hopping on the local Cinque Terre Express, which stops in all five villages. We had read about the Cinque Terre in our Rick Steves guidebook. It looked beautiful, and Greg was looking forward to pasta with pesto, which is what the area is famous for.

Sites and Bites

It was a relaxing five-hour ride with beautiful scenery, and we were able to grab a sandwich and a beer for lunch. My excitement level rose the closer we got! In my mind, we were going to get there, hang out at a local tavern, meet some locals who would invite us to stay in their adorable home, and charm the local chef into making us his specialty dish. I couldn't wait!

Eventually, we arrived at Riomaggiore, one of the five towns. It was afternoon, and it was hot! So hot. And the town was packed with tourists. I was very surprised. I didn't think that June was a high tourist season. Thank goodness we only had one piece of luggage each as we fought our way through the crowds. Riomaggiore was too busy, so we decided that we should visit one of the other towns along the coast.

Hopping on the Cinque Terre Express, we moved to another town. That, too, was busy. It looked like there were long lineups to get into any restaurant, so we went back on the train along with hundreds of other people. We went from town to town, getting off and getting back on, hoping the crowds would thin out. How were we supposed to find that local gem for our accommodation with so many people about? And why was it so hot?

Cinque Terre Sleepover

Repeatedly going back and forth between the towns, I started to recognize some of the other people on the train. Apparently, we all watched the same Rick Steves programs and read the same book. We started to smile and nod to each other, commiserating with each other over the packed location and transportation. Over the course of several hours off and on the train, I was getting cranky, and Greg was just downright miserable. We finally got off the train back at our starting point. Talk about being unhappy. We had just spent several hours without visiting any of the towns, and we hadn't had anything to eat since our sandwich on the train from Rome. It was close to 6 pm, and we had a decision to make. Were we going to continue with this craziness or just leave and head to another city, like maybe Pisa?

As we were trying to decide what to do, a couple from the train showed up.

They didn't have any luck either and were considering leaving the Cinque Terre. The four of us plopped our luggage down and introduced ourselves.

Bill and Jen were from Manitoba, Canada, and Greg and I were living in Vancouver at the time, so we talked about home and how easy we all thought traveling would be with a Rick Steves guidebook.

Sitting on a stone wall for the next hour and discussing what a failure of a day it had been, we were approached by an Italian man who asked us if we needed a room. YES. YES. YES.

The four of us grabbed our bags and followed him behind a small building, down a back alley, up a four-stepped ladder, and through another back alley before our Italian friend stopped at a door. This was definitely not a hotel.

He took out his key and told us we would have to be quiet now. He opened the door so we could step into our accommodation and I was very surprised to see a bed with someone having a siesta on it. We moved through this room to another door and went into a large bedroom. The room had a king-size bed and a set of twin bunk beds. The man advised that this was our room and asked if we wanted it. Exhausted from our day, all four of us said yes and paid the man cash for two nights' accommodations.

We now had to decide which couple would get the king-sized bed and which couple would get the bunks. Rock, paper, scissors decided it and Greg and I had the bunks. As our Italian landlord was leaving with our money, he said, "Oh yes, one more thing. I have already rented out the bottom bunk, so someone else will be here later tonight."

Cinque Terre Sleepover

Then he closed the door and was gone. Greg and I looked at each other, and I thought, *what the hell just happened? How on earth were two adults supposed to share a twin mattress?* Of course, Bill and Jen didn't care; they would be sleeping on the king-sized bed tonight.

It was now 8 pm, and our only other option for accommodation was to get back on the train, go to another location, and start looking for a place to stay for the night. Exhausted, frustrated, and hungry, Greg and I tossed our bags on the top bunk and left the room with our Canadian bunkmates in search of dinner.

Dinner in Italy starts much later than in Canada, so we were happy that the restaurants were still serving it, and because of the late hour, the day tourists had gone, making it easy to get a table. The four of us enjoyed a delicious meal that included focaccia, mussels, pesto Genovese with homemade pasta, and red wine. Lots of red wine.

After dinner, we bought a couple more bottles of red wine and then sat on the rocks by the sea. The four of us spent hours talking, laughing, and singing on the rocks. What a great way to end a really rough day. Of course, we weren't finished.

We made our way back to the room, and to this day, I'm not sure how we found it; we were all quite tipsy. As we tiptoed through the first room to access our shared bedroom, we were not as quiet as we thought. The four of us were trying to shush each other, which led to a lot of drunken giggles. Trying very hard to be respectful of the man already sleeping in our room, we didn't turn on the bedroom light. Bedtime for Bill and Jen was easy; they just went to the large bed and crawled in. But not for Greg and I. We had to figure out how to get onto the top bunk.

Greg climbed up first, the bed creaking and groaning the whole time. Then it was my turn. I'm not that agile to begin with, so climbing onto a top bunk in the dark after lots of red wine wasn't easy. My first attempt saw me missing the second step on the ladder and left me holding on to the bed, laughing and trying not to. The whole bed frame was shaking. Across the room, I could hear giggles. I tried again and still had no success. Greg was moving around on the top, trying to help, which didn't help the creaking sounds. More giggles and stumbles later, I was up on the bed, squished in closer to anyone than ever before in my life, while Greg and I tried to get comfortable on the twin-sized mattress. It was well after 1 am before I dropped off to sleep.

Cinque Terre Sleepover

Waking earlier than I wanted the next morning, I got up for a glass of water and saw that our lower bunk mate was already gone. To this day, I feel horrible for him having to experience us coming into the room so late and my drunken fumbles into the bunk. I hope that wherever he is, he can laugh at that night.

That day, we split off, and I don't know what Bill and Jen got up to, but Greg and I hiked the trail between the towns. It was fabulous, and I highly recommend it. Our last night was easier as we didn't have to worry about waking up another person, and I slipped into the bottom bunk for a good night's sleep.

The following morning, before checking out, I used the shower. On the wall of the shower was a huge red button the size of a dinner plate. I pushed it to see what would happen, but nothing did. I pushed it again, and still nothing. I finished showering and let the others use the shower.

After leaving the room, we enjoyed our last coffee together as a group, and we all started talking about the red button in the shower. It turns out we all pushed it multiple times. Finally, we all agreed that it was probably an emergency button in case someone slipped and fell. We said goodbye to Bill and Jen, and then Greg and I boarded another train to our next destination. As we were speeding along the track, I thought, *wait. If that was an emergency button, why did no one come to help?* To this day, I have no idea what the strange red button was.

CHAPTER 8

Beary Scary

Both grizzly bears and black bears live in British Columbia, and over the years, I've seen many of them. And while I love watching and photographing them, I also have huge respect for their power and always ensure I don't approach them too closely. I've been fortunate enough to observe grizzlies in the wild during the salmon spawning season as well as in Canada's national parks. Black bears seem to thrive wherever humans hang out, and I've seen bears while camping, hiking, and the odd time on a golf course.

So I felt a sense of excitement, not fear, when I learned there were bears in the area when I was visiting my

Sites and Bites

family in New Denver. Located on the east shore of Slocan Lake, in the West Kootenay region of British Columbia, this quaint town is picturesque and surrounded by forest. We came from all over the province for a family reunion.

Everyone had booked different accommodations for the four-day reunion, but the main gathering point was in the campground. My parents had booked a site and were there with their fifth-wheel trailer with a full kitchen. Everyone would gather at their campsite, and we would sit around the campfire, eat, drink, and laugh. Because New Denver is so small, walking distances were only 10 minutes, which made it perfect for enjoying a couple of beers and walking back to my room.

My dog Buddy was with me. He is a 70-pound Labrador who needs a ton of exercise, and walking to the campground wasn't enough, so we would walk the local forested trails twice daily.

One morning, my aunt sent a text saying, "Mama bear and her two young were in a tree at the end of Main Street." I grabbed Buddy and my camera and away we went to see.

Sure enough, there was a mama bear in a tree with her two cubs. All three were munching leaves, not caring

Beary Scary

about the people below them taking photographs. I took a few shots, but the bears were fairly hidden by the foliage. I wanted to get a different angle; however, I thought better of it since I didn't want Buddy or the bears to react to each other. I stood there for about 15 minutes just watching before Buddy and I took off along the lakeside nature trail.

The lakeside trail was stunning, following the shoreline of Slocan Lake. I kept Buddy close to me as I didn't know what kind of wildlife we would encounter, but we only saw a few chipmunks and birds. I saw bear droppings, so I knew bears used the trail. Two hours later, we were back at the cabin and ready to head down to the campground for more family fun.

The day was spent in the campground, eating, drinking, and laughing while everyone's dogs played and snoozed. A quick visit to the lake for the dogs to splash, then back to the campsite. As dusk approached, we all noticed three bears in the grassy area of the campground. I was so excited to see them. Of course, at this time, I didn't have my camera with a long lens and didn't manage to get any photos, but it was still fun to watch the bears wander about. They didn't seem concerned about people and didn't wander over to our campground where we were eating. After a while, it was too dark to see the

Sites and Bites

bears, but we could hear them crashing about in the forest area.

At some point in the evening, I called it a night. My brother and his wife were staying at the same motel I was in, so the three of us, along with Buddy, walked back in the pitch-dark. No one thought twice about the bears. It was such a beautiful walk; there must have been a million stars in the sky, and it was completely silent. This wasn't something I experienced while living in Vancouver.

The following morning, Buddy and I headed to the campground, but instead of going straight there, we took the forest trail along the creek leading to the lake and campground. Knowing that it was early enough for wildlife to be out, I was on the lookout for bears and other animals. My camera was ready, but to my disappointment, we saw nothing moving. Buddy had a great time sniffing and running.

I spent another great day visiting with family and throwing balls for the dogs. At some point in the early afternoon, I took Buddy for a walk in the forest, where I let him off-leash for a run before heading back to my room for some quiet time and a quick nap. Since this was our last night together, I suspected it would be a late

Beary Scary

night with several beers and cocktails, and I wanted to be fresh for the party.

Eventually, Buddy and I walked back to party central in the campground. We took the forest trail so Buddy could have an enjoyable walk. Since it was dusk and there were bears in the area, I didn't want to be in the forest for too long, so about halfway through our walk, I left the forest to walk down one of the residential streets, feeling this would be safer.

I was walking in the middle of the street, just looking at houses and gardens, while Buddy sniffed the bushes. Suddenly, I heard yelling. I looked up the street and saw this guy sitting in his car yelling at me. "Hey," he said. "There's a bear!" and sure enough, there was a black bear in a garden about 15 feet away. I hadn't even seen it.

I stopped, not knowing what to do. I was a block from the campsite where everyone was gathering, but I would have to walk past the bear to get there. I could go back, but that would put me back in the forest, and I was seriously concerned about running into bears there, too. The guy in the car drove off, so I had no help there if I needed it. I was frozen with indecision. Buddy still had not noticed the bear.

Sites and Bites

While I was standing there trying to decide what to do, the bear stood up on his hind legs to get a better look at me. He was huge! And he let out a sound that raised the hair on the back of my neck and left me shivering. I stood there for what seemed like hours but was probably minutes before the bear dropped back to all fours and went back to foraging in the garden.

By now, Buddy knew the bear was there, and he was shivering, his tail tucked between his legs. I shortened his leash, moved to the far side of the street, and marched quickly past the bear, not looking back, praying it wasn't coming after us. Thankfully, the bear took no further interest in us.

I reached the campground safely but couldn't enjoy myself. All I could think about was the bear. How was I going to get back to my room safely? If I had not seen the bear when it was still light out, how would I have seen it in the pitch dark?

I explained my dilemma to my family, and they all decided to walk me and Buddy to the lit highway so I could go back. Safety in numbers was the thought.

Buddy and I made it safely to our room, and I spent the rest of the night and the entire drive back to Vancouver

Beary Scary

questioning every decision I had ever made to hike with just my dog. I thought I knew the bear risk, but clearly, I was just fooling myself. The sound that the bear made has bothered me to this day, and many months later, I still haven't gone walking in the woods alone.

Sites and Bites

City Sculpture

Gallery

Breakfast at Pepe's

Sites and Bites

Family Fun in Mexico

Fun in Spain

Gallery

Gates of the Taj Mahal

Indian Architecture

Sites and Bites

Vancouver's Steam Clock

Gallery

Wild Grizzly

CHAPTER 9

Pig Snout Drama

Cádiz, Spain, one of the oldest continuously inhabited cities in Europe, is located on a narrow peninsula jutting out into the Atlantic Ocean. The city boasts an impressive history dating back over 3,000 years with influences from Roman, Moorish, and Spanish cultures. The city is surrounded by water on three sides, ensuring it has multiple options for those who love the beach or just taking in views of the Atlantic Ocean. Cádiz is famous for its many colourful and fun festivals throughout the year. So of course I would want to visit this historic city.

My husband and I were vacationing in Spain with another family, and we had rented a house for all of us to stay in.

Sites and Bites

The wonderful part of renting a house with close friends is that it allows everyone to do what they want and to visit places that are interesting to them while still having a place to meet up at the end of the day. Some days, both families visited sites or areas together, and other days, we would split off into different groups.

The day that Greg and I decided to visit Cádiz, we took our son, Denby, and his friend Aksel. This would be an all-day adventure as our destination was a three-hour drive. Both boys were 12 years old, and I knew that we couldn't excite them just by going to see Spain's oldest city, so I told them we were going in search of geckos. I had researched and found a spot close to Cádiz that apparently boasted a large population of these creatures.

Due to the long drive, we left the rental house early and away we went. A couple of hours later, we reached the location where we all expected to see hundreds of geckos. Denby and Aksel looked everywhere as we wandered around, and after an hour of searching, we had only counted five geckos. The boys were very disappointed when we left to continue our journey.

Our next stop was Sanlúcar, and Greg and I decided it was a good place to stop and take a walk along the beach. A parking spot was difficult to find, but eventually, we found

Pig Snout Drama

a spot a few blocks from the beach. To ensure we could find our car later, the four of us walked in a straight line to the beach, and within a couple of minutes, we came to a beach snack shack. Greg told Denby and Aksel that if, for some reason, we got separated, they were to head for the beach shack and stay there until we came to get them.

We spent the next hour walking along the beach, with the boys running around and splashing in the water. We even found a plaque that told us this was the location where Christopher Columbus set sail for the New World on his third trip.

Eventually, we turned back. After all, we still had to get to Cádiz. We walked back to the beach shack and turned up the street to our car. Ten minutes later, we still had not found it. We walked around and around looking for our car or for something that we recognized, to no avail. Deciding that the best bet would be to head back to the beach and the beach shack marker so we could start over, we turned back.

Upon returning to the beach, we noticed something that we hadn't seen before. There was more than one beach shack, and they all looked the same! I'm not sure how we could've missed this. The boys were thirsty, so we grabbed them a drink while Greg and I tried to figure out which beach shack was our marker. We got lucky, and our second try successfully got us back to our car, and we headed to Cádiz. No more pit stops.

We spent the afternoon exploring the maze-like streets of the Old Town, visiting the ancient fortifications, and admiring the stunning architecture. Cádiz's past includes watchtowers, and today, there are still over 100 still standing. Camera Obscura, an optical illusion display overlooking the city, is housed in one of the watchtowers. Denby wanted to visit Camera Obscura and see if it was comparable to the one we had visited in Edinburgh the previous year.

Up the tower we went to explore and participate in the optical illusions on display. Both boys loved the experience, but the highlight was when we were on the rooftop of the old watchtower. From the top, we were looking down on the city streets and buildings, and we could see a man on the patio of a lower building hanging up his laundry. The unusual part? He was wearing nothing but a pair of shoes! This was enough to send a couple of 12-year-old boys into giggles.

Shortly after the entertaining view, we left the tower and headed back to the winding streets. We were all hungry and started wandering through the historic center, looking

Pig Snout Drama

for a place to eat. As we wandered, we heard music and followed it until we came upon a restaurant with outside seating. Deciding that listening to live music from a local musician would be a nice addition to lunch, we grabbed a table.

We didn't speak Spanish, and the waiter didn't speak English, so we mimed to each other and got our drink orders. The waiter managed to ask us, "English menu?" but we refused. Even though we didn't speak the language, we were confident that between the four of us, we could figure out the menu; it was part of the fun. We ordered four small plates and waited with excitement to see what we had ordered.

It turns out we had ordered some dishes that were very unusual for us. We had fried fish, oxtail stew, and pork snout. The fish and the stew were ok, but the pig snout had us all pausing. It was cut into square chunks with a sauce on it. But, because we travel to expand our experiences, we all grabbed a fork and dug in.

I bit into it, but the texture wasn't appealing, and I couldn't seem to swallow it. I politely spit it into my napkin. Denby also spit his bite out. Greg and Aksel did much better; they both swallowed their bite, but we all decided that this was not a dish for us and left the rest. Despite the unusual food, we still enjoyed the rest of the meal and the local entertainment. Soon, it was time to go; we still had a three-hour drive back to the house.

As we wandered back to the car, I noticed that Denby and Aksel were hanging back a bit. I turned to tell them to hurry up when I saw Aksel barfing on the street. Apparently, lunch didn't sit well with him. But like any self-respecting child, by the time we made it back to the car, he had recovered enough to ask for an ice-cream cone for the trip home.

The drive back was very quiet, with the boys sleeping in the backseat, Greg driving, and me trying to figure out how I was going to tell my friend that we had gotten lost, fed her son something that made him throw up, and had exposed him to a naked person. All in all, it was a very adventurous day.

CHAPTER 10

Cocolalla Cabin

I had been dating Greg for several years before I discovered that his family owned a cabin on Cocolalla Lake in northern Idaho between Coeur d'Alene and Sandpoint. One night, the two of us were out with a bunch of friends having beers, and Greg suggested a road trip and a long weekend at the cabin. Everyone drunkenly thought this was a great idea.

We planned the road trip for two weekends out and made sure that we had time off work. Thursday night after work, everyone gathered at Greg's place as we convoyed to the cabin. The driving time from Vancouver, BC, to the lake was seven hours and 45 minutes. Quite a drive for a long weekend. There were 10 of us in four cars as we headed to the border, crossing into Washington State. Immediately on the southern side of the Canadian/American border, we stopped at the first gas station, where we filled up our gas tanks and grabbed road trip snacks and drinks. And we were off.

We headed south on I-5 toward Seattle before turning off onto the 405 S toward Spokane. In the car I was driving, Greg and his friend Doug were sitting in the backseat, and my friend Jenny Lynn was in the passenger seat. We were rocking to 80s music, singing and laughing. We had been driving for a little over six hours, and it was close to midnight when Jenny Lynn said she needed to use the washroom. Thankfully, a few minutes later, we saw a sign for a pub and pulled in.

The pub was small, dimly lit, and packed with people. I can only assume they were locals, as this pub didn't appear to be attached to a town or community. The boys bellied up to the bar for a beer, and Jen (short for Jenny Lynn) and I made our way to the bathroom.

I've never seen such a bathroom. There were two bathrooms, single toilets and sinks. But what made them so unusual was the star-shaped cut-out on each wooden door. If anyone was outside the door, they would be able

Cocolalla Cabin

to see the person inside using the toilet. Jen and I took turns blocking the view.

Another unusual thing about the stall was the bright orange shag carpet on the ceiling. I was glad to get out as this bathroom just didn't feel clean to me. It's still a wonder as to the purpose of the carpeted ceiling and cutout.

We loaded back into the car, and I continued to drive until we found the turnoff for the lake. It was now close to 2 am, and it was pitch black as I slowly drove down the gravel road, looking for the sign to the cabin. It felt a bit spooky, but finally, we arrived safe and sound. We staked out a bed and waited for the others to join us before everyone crashed for the rest of the night.

Early the next morning, several people headed into Sandpoint for groceries and alcohol. Apparently, preparing for the weekend at the cabin didn't include any of us bringing anything to eat. While some shopped, Greg got the boat and the dock into the lake.

The next few days were fabulous. The hot July days were perfect for boating, waterskiing, and canoeing. The first afternoon, a couple of our friends, Julie and Joan, canoed across the lake and came back with some exciting news.

There was a campground just a few minutes away, and the campground had a bar. We agreed to visit the bar after dinner that night.

In the dark, we walked the gravel road to the campground bar and introduced ourselves to Gail, the bartender. This tiny pub was big enough to hold a pool table, a jukebox, three tables for customers, a small dance floor, and eight bar stools at the counter, but it was packed with standing room only when we got there. We joined the locals and campers playing pool and danced ourselves silly.

At one point during the night, I went to the bar for another drink. I was drinking Kahlua and milk. Gail poured a heavy serving of Kahlua before realizing there was no milk left. Before I could change my drink order, Gail picked up the Baileys and proceeded to fill my glass with that instead of milk. I must have had about eight ounces of alcohol in that drink. This was now my go-to drink for the remainder of the night.

An hour later, someone started buying shooters; the house special was a very strange-looking blue concoction, but we drank them. When it was my turn to buy the shots, I went to the bar and told Gail I would like four house shooters.

Cocolalla Cabin

She told me that it would be $10. My friend Cindy yelled across the bar, "Get two more." So, I added that to my order. As Gail poured the shots, she quoted me $8 for the drinks. What? Was I hearing correctly? The price went down? I added four more shots to the order for a total of 10 shooters, and Gail quoted me $6. I left the counter with 10 shooters for $6. Unheard of. This now became the group drink for the remainder of the night.

As you can imagine, the following morning was very slow as everyone slept late except for me. Trying to be quiet, I grabbed a couple of beers, a bowl of chips, my book and headed to the water. The morning was beautiful. I climbed into the boat, read my book, and drank my beers until some friends made their way down to the boat around 9:30 in the morning. We spent the morning boating, tubing, and swimming before I eventually went for a siesta on the shaded porch.

Late afternoon had everyone back on the lake, but now the super soakers were out, adult style. Instead of shooting water at each other, we were shooting blackberry vodka. Needless to say, this was messy, and we were all quite tipsy by the time we headed back to the campground bar. Our favourite bartender, Gail, was at work, and we ordered cocktails and put money in the jukebox. As the evening wore on, I noticed that every time someone

Sites and Bites

ordered shots, Gail would take a shot of cinnamon snaps. She was partying with the rest of us. I'm not sure what time the bar was supposed to close, but we partied there until just before dawn.

That morning was quiet around the cabin, with most people sleeping in, and those who did wake up weren't very energetic. That afternoon, along with our friends Randy and Doug, Greg and I went to the campground for an afternoon drink. Gail was there again. I'm not sure if she owned the bar, but she appeared to be the only person who worked there.

Inside the bar was a customer sitting on one of the stools, and his dog was sitting on one of the other stools. The guys stepped up to the bar and, after some discussion, ordered Cognac in heated glasses. Gail didn't know how to heat the glasses, but before the guys could change their drink order, Gail dropped their glasses into the deep fryer for a quick second and then poured in the alcohol. How bizarre. I hadn't ordered a drink yet but was standing at the end of the counter when the other customer started talking to us, asking where we were from.

At some point in the conversation, I mentioned that I loved that his dog was able to sit on a bar stool. He said, "That's not the only trick he can do." The man then

Cocolalla Cabin

reached into his coat pocket and pulled out a lipstick tube. He proceeded to put the lipstick on and said to his dog, "Kisses." The dog leaned over and licked the lipstick off the man's mouth. This was the strangest bar I had ever been in. At that point, I left the bar and went back to the cabin. Later that night, after dinner, we all went back to the campground bar for more dancing, playing pool, and weird drinks.

Our last day was spent tubing and waterskiing in the morning before closing up the cabin and making the long trek back to Vancouver. Everyone had so much fun that a long weekend trip to Cocolalla became an annual tradition for the next decade.

CHAPTER 11

Las Vegas Baby

I still remember my first visit to Las Vegas. Greg, who was my boyfriend at the time, and I were staying at his family's cabin in northern Idaho for two weeks for summer vacation. The only bump in our vacation was three days when we couldn't access the cabin as it was promised to others. We searched for something easy and inexpensive to do, and our search results kept leading us to Las Vegas. It seemed we were destined to go there, so I booked a flight from Spokane (a short drive from the cabin) to Vegas and away we went.

To say I was overwhelmed by the sounds and lights of Las Vegas is an understatement. We caught a taxi from the airport to our hotel, and when the cab driver dropped us off, I thought he had made a mistake. Greg and I entered the front doors and stepped directly into the casino. The sounds of the slot machines made it seem like everyone was winning huge jackpots.

We stood there for a few minutes trying to figure out how to find the front of our hotel when we realized that the hotel check-in desk was at the far end of the slot machines. Dragging our luggage through the casino, we arrived at reception, where the keys to our room were quickly provided, and our adventure began.

For the next three days, we wandered The Strip during the day and at night, and I saw more lights and neon signs than I could ever have imagined. There were so many that the night was almost as bright as midday. No wonder Vegas is called the "Neon Capital of the World"!

We gambled at the slot machines and roulette tables, ate at the cheap buffets, drank free cocktails, and went to a couple of shows. I'm pretty sure we never slept more than six hours the entire trip. Of course, three days isn't even close to enough time to discover all that Las Vegas has to offer and a return trip would have to be made in the future.

Las Vegas Baby

So a few years later, when my good friend Katherine called and asked if I thought a girls' weekend in Vegas was a good idea, I said, "Absolutely!" Katherine was amazing. She organized the group of six by booking the rooms and the flights, and a few short weeks later, it was departure day.

I showed up at the airport only to realize that I couldn't find my email with the flight information. I didn't think to print it because I would have my phone with me. I wasn't worried, though; I thought I would just find the flight leaving Vancouver to go to Las Vegas that day and provide my passport at check in.

Was I ever surprised when I saw the flight schedule. Not only were there several flights to Vegas leaving around the same time, but they were also on multiple airlines. I called Katherine's cell without luck. I waited a few minutes and tried again. No answer.

After thinking about it for a couple of minutes, I decided that the only reasonable thing to do would be to scan my passport at each airline's check-in kiosk until I was successful. I started with the one immediately in front of me without luck, so I moved on to the second airline's kiosk and scanned my passport. Nope. I didn't have a seat on this airline. I moved on to the third option.

Then, the fourth. The fifth airline was the winner. I had a seat booked on that flight, so I checked in and went through security. It still surprises me that no one stopped me while I was searching and scanning my passport in multiple locations.

I met my friends at the departure gate, and we were off! The six of us shared three rooms for four nights, and we spent the first two days together gambling, shopping, and lying beside the pool. On day three, I begged off when the girls wanted to go shopping again. I'm not much of a shopper, so when they left, I made my way back to a favourite casino and slot machine. I dropped a hundred dollars in and played for about 40 minutes when I won a $3500 jackpot. I was so excited I kissed the old guy beside me, tipped the waitress, and decided to take myself out to a celebratory lunch.

I found a cute restaurant in The Forum Shops at Caesars Place and ordered a fancy bottle of wine to go with lunch. Because I was alone, I was sitting at the bar eating, drinking, and reading a book I had picked up along the way from the casino to the restaurant. By the time I had finished my lunch, a couple of guys had sat down next to me, drinking beers and eating. Soon, they started talking to me, and we had fun talking about sports and hometowns. Even though I had just

Las Vegas Baby

finished a bottle of wine, I was enjoying myself, so I ordered another glass.

At some point, I guess these guys realized that I was quite tipsy and decided to see if they could swap bar bills with me. They figured I was an easy mark. I quickly agreed. Of course, the nice bartender tried to intervene on my behalf (which I thought was so awesome), but I assured him that I was perfectly content to exchange bills. It was clear to me that the bartender didn't like what was happening, but he went and grabbed the bills for both parties. He looked at the bar tabs, quickly looked up at me, and started laughing.

He presented me with the bill for the guys; it had six beers and two hamburgers. I paid for it and left him a nice tip. Then he gave my bill to the two guys. My fancy bottle of wine, which they didn't know about, was three times their lunch tab, and of course, there were also other glasses of wine and lunch on the tab. The two guys started raising a ruckus and saying they weren't paying for it. The bartender advised that they would pay for it, as they had agreed to the swap, or the police would be called.

Grudgingly, they paid and then angrily stomped off without saying goodbye to me. The bartender was still laughing when he said to me, "Clever girl." I gave him a

Sites and Bites

kiss on the cheek and thanked him for helping to make my afternoon a delight. That night, along with my friends, I continued to gamble and party in Las Vegas style.

The following day was our last, and we walked The Strip, rode the roller coaster in New York, New York, gambled, and spent more time at the pool. On our last night, one of my friends wanted to go to a new nightclub opening, so we all got dressed up and made our way there.

At some point in the evening, I decided that I had enough clubbing and made my way back to our hotel. My friend Katherine was playing blackjack in the casino bar. I joined her, and we played for a while before an older guy sat down beside her. Katherine and I both thought that he looked like Fidel Castro. Knowing that he couldn't actually be Fidel, we laughed and giggled about it anyway, and as always seems to happen, Fidel started talking to us. There we were, the three of us playing blackjack, drinking, and having fun.

Eventually, our new friend "Fidel" stood between Katherine and me while we gambled and drank. I'm quite an animated person when I'm drinking, so while I was laughing and talking, I was moving about and waving my hands around a lot. At one point, I pointed to my blackjack hand so Katherine could see what my

Las Vegas Baby

latest hand looked like, and Fidel leaned over me to see as well.

Katherine said something funny, and without realizing where he was, I laughed so hard that I whipped my head back. Unfortunately, Fidel was directly in the path of my head, and I ended up cracking his nose. After making sure that he was OK, Katherine and I decided that it was a good time to call it a night and off to our room we went.

The following morning, we just had time for a bit of relaxation by the pool before heading to the airport. Three nights in Vegas never seems like enough, but our four-night trip was way too long. I was glad to be going home.

CHAPTER 12

Bikinis and Socks in Hawaii

The first time I went to Hawaii, I was 18. I was very excited to go as this was my first vacation outside my country. The two-week trip was with my mom and aunt, who I was very close to. We were all excited to have a girls' trip in a beautiful location, but it didn't end up as peaceful as we would've liked.

The trip started out ok; our flight was smooth with no delays, the check-in at the hotel went well, and we were situated a short walk through the

International Marketplace to the beach. Upon arrival, we unpacked and then grabbed a bite to eat for dinner, eager for the following day so we could hang out on the famous Waikiki Beach.

We were all up early on our first full day in paradise. With our beach bags packed with essentials like water, sunscreen, books, and towels, we made our way through the busy market selling a ton of puka shell necklaces and grabbed a spot on the sand.

That day was a typical tourist in Hawaii day. We spent time on the beach, swam in the waves, had our pictures taken with tropical birds (for an outrageous price), and went on a catamaran in the afternoon. A quick meal that night ended the first perfect day of our perfect vacation.

Unfortunately, perfection didn't last. Day two started out the same as day one, but I apparently didn't put enough sunscreen on this time. After seven hours of laying in the sun, I ended up with a very bad burn on both arms. I was in need of first aid for my burn. Along with Aunt Judy and Mom, we left the beach in search of a store that sold Solarcaine. It took about 30 minutes, but we found the shop we needed and made our purchase. Because of my burn, I was sore and cranky, so we headed back to our hotel room, ordered dinner, and called it a night.

Bikinis and Socks in Hawaii

The following morning found me crying; my arms were so red and hurting, but as we all wanted to head to the beach, I slopped on a double amount of sunscreen, and we headed out. Unfortunately, the sun was so strong that even the sunscreen wasn't enough. I could feel the burn worsening. There wasn't a single area of shade, and I knew I wouldn't be able to stay on the beach that day. Thankfully, Judy and Mom were accommodating, and we dropped off our beach gear at our hotel room and decided that today would be our shopping day. We spent the day going from shop to shop just looking around, and I was able to stay in the shade and in the air-conditioned shops.

Feeling better the following day, I got ready for the beach again, and the three of us headed back to the sand. My arms were still very burnt, but I was determined to get back to the beach. Within an hour, I knew I needed something to cover my arms. We went back to the shops but couldn't find any shirts with long sleeves. Then, my mom had a great idea. She purchased long white sports socks and proceeded to cut holes in the toes so I could wear them like gloves. For the next several days, I was on the beach wearing my string bikini and my over-the-elbow sock gloves. I'm sure I was quite the sight. Problem solved, I was able to enjoy myself on the beach.

Sites and Bites

One day, the three of us were just hanging out and people-watching when we saw the most unusual sight. A very tall, tanned, and fit man was walking down the beach wearing a lime green thong bathing suit with lime green suspenders. Talk about eye-catching! It was my favorite look of the trip.

One afternoon, Judy told us that she had bought tickets for an evening boat cruise to watch the sunset. That sounded like so much fun, and as we made our way to the boat, I wished I had brought my camera so I could take pictures; unfortunately, I had left it at the hotel.

Turns out this was a good thing. Judy, Mom, and I loaded onto the boat with about a hundred other people and were handed our welcome drink. It was a very strong rum-based fruit punch. As we sailed on the ocean, it became very clear that we weren't on a sunset cruise but a booze cruise! The music was loud, the punch was flowing, and everyone was dancing. It was so exciting!

Several hours later, I was swaying down the walkway with everyone else, and we loaded onto several tour buses. My mom kept asking Judy if this was part of the ticketed event, but Judy had no idea. After about a 10-minute drive, everyone got off the buses and entered a nightclub for more free cocktails and lots of dancing until the wee hours.

Bikinis and Socks in Hawaii

Around 3 am, Judy, Mom, and I left the club and started walking in what we all hoped was the right direction to our hotel. At some point, Judy tripped on a sloped curb, stumbled, and went down. She had ripped her pants and the following morning would see a huge bruise on her knee. Eventually, we reached our room, crawled into bed, and slept late. I'm not sure about anyone else, but I had a wee hangover.

Two days later, we joined a guided hike up Diamond Head Crater. We met at the designated starting point, and as we stood there with a couple dozen other people, our tour guide started handing out garbage bags and latex gloves. What? She explained that part of the guided tour was picking up garbage as we walked. My mom declined to take a garbage bag, explaining that she signed up for a guided tour, not garbage detail. That appeared to make the guide angry, and she refused to speak to the three of us or answer any of our questions about the area we were walking through.

After about 30 minutes of this, the three of us decided to leave the tour and hike to the top of the crater on our own. What a gorgeous trail! The view was beautiful, but one thing we were learning about Waikiki was there didn't seem to be any shade anywhere. Our entire hike was in the sun, and stupidly, none of us had hats or brought any water. By the time we got to the top of the hike, we were very, very thirsty.

At the viewpoint were a couple of guys drinking beers. We were prepared to pay any price for a beer, but that was when we discovered that none of us had even brought our wallets. Thankfully, the guys were nice enough to give us a bottle of water, which we gulped down. A long, hot hike back down the crater and to our hotel room ended that day; no one wanted dinner, just more water.

The day we had tickets for an island tour that ended with a luau was gorgeous, and we boarded our bus with enthusiasm. We spent several hours on board while the driver drove around the island and pointed out interesting and beautiful sights. Part of the tour included lunch and drinks, so we were served sandwiches and a drink called a Blue Hawaiian. It was delicious, and I had several. As the day turned into evening, our tour driver took us to the Polynesian Cultural Center for our luau.

The following day, Judy and Mom kept talking about the luau; they both thought the meal was fun and loved the fire dance when the sun went down. Fire dance? I had no idea. I didn't even remember much after arriving at the cultural center, never mind a fire dance. Apparently, the Blue Hawaiians I was drinking all afternoon packed a huge punch. That night is a big blank for me.

By the time our vacation was coming to an end, I was ready to head home. I was exhausted. Our last day was to be spent on the beach, just chilling. For some reason, Judy took a look at our return tickets, and it was a good thing that she did. Mom and I were packing our beach bag, ready for one more day on the beach, but Judy stopped us. We were all wrong. Today was the day of our departure, and we had only a couple of hours before our flight home. Scrambling, we changed clothes, packed our bags, grabbed a cab, and somehow made our flight home.

CHAPTER 13

Breakfast at Pepe's

My husband, son, and I had rented a house in Oliva, Spain, and we shared it for two weeks with our good friends, Doug and Arlyn and their daughter, Charlie. The house had a pool and was a quick five-minute walk to the beach.

Greg, Denby, and I arrived at the house first, and as we entered the community and headed toward our house, we drove by a cute restaurant. It turns out this restaurant was only 500 metres from our rental house. How perfect.

We claimed our bedrooms, unpacked our bags and decided to walk to the restaurant for lunch. The Spanish we spoke was extremely limited, and it appeared that the wait staff didn't speak any English, so communicating was difficult, but eventually, we realized there was no menu. We ordered what we believed to be the meal of the day and waited.

Our waitress brought over two glasses of white wine, a Coke, and three bowls of soup. She then brought over a huge salad for the table. Then, she brought two orders of a fish dish and an omelette (the one thing I knew how to order). When we finished all the food, she steered Denby, who was 12, inside the restaurant, where he could pick out an ice-cream bar from the freezer. Denby ate his ice cream while Greg and I ordered a second glass of wine. The total cost for our lunch was $20. This restaurant, named Pepe's, just became our new favourite spot.

Eventually, our friends arrived, and we settled in for our vacation. The six of us spent the next several days touring the area, hiking, and hanging out at several different beaches. One very hot day, we decided to just hang out at the house and pool. Lunch was just a short walk to Pepe's; delicious, inexpensive, and easy.

One day, I decided I wanted to get some sunrise shots at the nearby beach, so I set my alarm for the following day and ensured my camera battery was charged. When the alarm rang the following morning at 5:30, I quickly

Breakfast at Pepe's

dressed, grabbed my camera, and walked down to the beach in the dark. The sun rose just after 6:00, and I managed to get a couple of really great shots. I noticed several people were out for a morning walk along the sand, and since I was there, I decided that was something I should do, too.

I spent an hour walking along the beach in one direction, which meant an hour of walking back, which normally wouldn't be a problem. However, Spain was hot. Hotter than I expected. By 8:00, it was already too hot for a brisk-paced walk. I was dripping with sweat.

Close to the house, I saw that Pepe's was open and full. Clearly, this was a favorite local hangout. As I was about to walk past the restaurant, a white, covered truck pulled up, and the driver jumped out and opened the doors at the back. The truck was packed full of fresh baked goods and loaves of bread. People jumped up from their tables to line up and purchase what he had for sale.

I had a couple of Euros in my pocket, so I lined up as well. I had enough money to buy a loaf of bread and six chocolate croissants. They were all still warm. Feeling pleased with my purchase, I continued home and let myself in to find that everyone else was still sleeping.

Sites and Bites

Since it was so hot, and I was feeling kind of yucky from my walk, I dove into the pool, clothes and all, and waited for the rest of the house to wake up.

The following day was a repeat for me: a walk in the dark, sunrise photos, a hot beach walk, and bread from the truck in front of Pepe's. This time, while waiting for my turn, I studied the people eating at Pepe's and noticed something I don't see in Canada. Almost every person had either a glass of wine or a glass of Cognac with their breakfast. It was only eight in the morning!

On the third sunrise walk, I decided to do the same as the locals. Before leaving the house that morning, I made sure I had some money and left a note for everyone telling them where I would be. Coming back from my walk, I sat down at an empty table, ordered an omelette and a glass of white wine, and just relaxed. It felt strangely decadent to be drinking wine so early in the morning, but it also felt like the right thing to do. I fit right in with everyone else.

Around 9:30, the rest of my family and friends showed up for breakfast and joined me for some wine. By the time we were done, I was ready for my first siesta of the day. During the rest of our trip, we continued to make our wine and breakfast pitstop at Pepe's, though none of us braved the Cognac so early in the day. Maybe on the next trip to Spain.

CHAPTER 14

Truck Stop Sleepover

One day, Greg and I decided that we should visit his Aunt Edna, who lived in Reno Nevada. We decided to drive At this point in time, we were in Sandpoint, Idaho, and we figured we could drive to Reno in a day. Clearly, we never looked up how far it actually was, but we packed our bags and left the house after a lazy breakfast. Not only did we not realize that the trip was 820 miles, but we didn't have GPS in our car, nor a map. I mean, how hard could it be? Just head south. The trip started out fun. The weather was warm, we had all the car windows open, and the music cranked. Road trip!

Sites and Bites

We left Sandpoint and headed south on the 95 toward Coeur d'Alene, where we stopped for gas and some snacks for the trip. Continuing on, we passed through Moscow, Lewiston, Cottonwood, and New Meadows. We were making great time. But somehow, at New Meadows, we managed to get off the main route and ended up taking a different road. This was a much smaller road, and we saw very few towns, but it was a very pretty and interesting drive until it started to get late in the day, and we were getting low on gas. At the first town where we wanted to stop and get gas, the station was closed. The next area we came to didn't appear to have a gas station.

Both of us were starting to feel stressed. What would we do if we ran out of gas? And where were we? There was nothing left to do but continue, so we did. We finally found an open Chevron in a place called Horseshoe Bend. We stopped, filled up our gas tank, took a quick bathroom break, and grabbed more water before moving on.

As we continued our road trip, we eventually came to Boise and saw signs for Highway 95. Finally, we were back on track. It was dark out at this point, but we figured we could make good time now that we had found the right road.

Truck Stop Sleepover

We were both tired and cranky, speeding along the highway, but we still had a long drive ahead of us. Driving hour after hour, Reno was still nowhere in sight. At some point, Greg said he was too tired to continue driving, so I started to look for signs for a hotel. I didn't have a driver's license, and Greg had been driving the entire trip. Another 45 minutes passed without any sign for accommodations, but we did see a sign for a truck stop, so we took that exit.

I had never stopped at a truck stop, so I was quite surprised at how big the facility was. A restaurant, gas station, shower facilities, and over 100 semitrailer trucks were parked in the area. Greg parked the car, we used the washroom facilities, and grabbed a burger for dinner. As we sat in the car eating, we discussed our options. There was just no use to continue driving as Greg was too tired, and since we had no idea where a hotel was, we decided to just sleep in the car where it was parked.

I didn't think I would be able to sleep with the noise of the trucks, but Greg and I drifted off to a deep sleep in spite of the noise, the lack of blankets, and the fact that we were sitting up. The following morning, we woke around eight, only to realize that our car was the only vehicle in the parking lot. Somehow, we slept so deeply that we missed every truck leaving the area.

But that was OK as we both felt rested, so we grabbed a coffee to go and started back on the highway. Greg drove for about 10 minutes before we saw a sign for Reno. We were five miles from the city limits. If we had known that last night, we would have continued to Aunt Edna's and a bed. Thirty minutes later, we knocked on her door for a surprise visit and a few days of relaxation before our return road trip.

CHAPTER 15

Road Trip with a Stranger

I was working as a cashier in Vancouver when I started to get itchy feet. I needed to go somewhere. Life had gotten too predictable. Since I didn't have a lot of money, a plane ticket was out of the question, and I decided a road trip was in my very near future.

The only question was, where did I want to go? I lived close enough to Kelowna and the Okanagan Valley that I had been there several times already. I had no desire to head north, and Alberta, the next closest province, held no appeal. So that meant south, into the United States.

Sites and Bites

But where south? And how long did I want to be driving? I carefully looked at maps for guidance. Washington State? Too close. Oregon? Nope, nothing jumped out at me. California? Maybe. The weather was good, and I was sure to enjoy my time. But then, as I continued to look at the map, I realized that if I could drive to California, I could drive to Arizona and the Grand Canyon, which was on my bucket list. Decision made, I started to make plans.

I booked time off work and tried to figure out the best driving route. Throughout the next two weeks, I was busy working, planning, and discussing my trip with friends and family. During this time, a strange thing happened. My family and friends were having a bit of a freakout about me road-tripping on my own. This would be my first time doing so, so I get it, but seriously, I was an adult after all.

One day, a few days before my vacation, I was working, and a close friend called me. They were expressing concern about me traveling alone. Didn't I know there was a serial killer in California? I tried to explain that I wouldn't even be in that part of the world, but they didn't hear me. Eventually, I hung up the phone so I could focus on work.

"I'll go with you," a voice said. I looked up from my work to see a co-worker looking at me. "I've been listening to

Road Trip with a Stranger

you plan your trip, and I would love to go on a road trip with you."

At first, I thought this was very weird. Even though Nadia was my co-worker, we hadn't really spent any time together, and I didn't know her at all. I told her I would think about it.

As the day wore on, I realized that traveling with her would provide my friends and family with some comfort that I wasn't alone, never mind that I'd be traveling with a stranger. I told Nadia I was happy to have her along, and we worked out the details.

I picked Nadia up at her house at 5 am, and we headed south toward the border. The goal was to drive until we hit Reno. Fifteen hours later, we had arrived. I was exhausted as I had driven the entire way and couldn't wait to get into my hotel room. The only problem was we didn't have a room booked. The night we arrived was a busy one in Reno, and it took us almost an hour to go from hotel to hotel before we managed to secure one for the night.

I was ready to just chill for the night, but this is when I learned a bit about my traveling companion. Nadia wanted to go out and see the sights. She pushed me until I agreed, and the two of us walked around the city for several hours, visiting the casinos, having dinner at a truck stop diner, poking our noses into the sex shops, and drinking at a couple of bars. By the time we made it back to our hotel room, I could barely stand up, so I fell into bed and was sleeping immediately. The next morning, despite how tired I was, we were up and in the car by 6 am.

Our trip today would find us ending in Las Vegas. This was going to be a short drive compared to the day before, only seven hours between cities. Nadia and I shared the driving as I still needed some sleep. I'm sure the drive was beautiful, but due to my exhaustion, I was unable to appreciate the dry desert landscape. There were a couple of interesting things to note. The amount of land that was restricted access only was shocking to me. I have no idea what was behind all that fencing, but the harsh warning signs were enough to squelch my curiosity.

Another interesting thing we came across was a school bus brothel. Coming from Vancouver, brothels weren't the norm and I was quite fascinated by the fact that there were signs directing traffic to the school bus. It was also very strange to see an old school bus parked on the side of the road being used as the entrance to a brothel. I wanted to stop and take a couple of pictures, but the two of us decided that was probably not the best idea, so we moved on.

Road Trip with a Stranger

Hours later, we arrived in Las Vegas and had the same issue as Reno. No booked accommodation. We went from hotel to hotel, but they were all full. Apparently, arriving in Las Vegas on a Friday night without a room wasn't a smart idea; everything was booked. As we sat in our car, parked on a side road, a man approached us and asked if we needed a place to stay. He said he had some room in student housing if we wanted a room. We quickly agreed, paid him, and he gave us a key and directions to the building. As I drove to the apartment block, Nadia and I started to laugh. We both thought we had just been ripped off $50. To our delight, we arrived at a very clean apartment building and let ourselves into the suite.

As we did in Reno, we set out to explore the city right away. We walked for hours, hitting the casinos in downtown Vegas, drinking boozy slushies, and just enjoying the sights before heading back to bed. The next leg of our trip was only a four-hour drive, so we slept in a bit and then explored Vegas some more.

We left Vegas for Flagstaff after an early dinner, and it was dark by the time we arrived. Again, we had no reservations anywhere. We went from hotel to hotel, but the hotels were outrageously priced. I think the hotel clerks realized we were exhausted, so they could up the price of rooms. Our final stop was a hotel where the manager offered

Nadia the option of free room and board if we wanted to stay with him. Yuck.

Looking at each other, we decided to just sleep in the car in one of the hotel parking lots, and that's what we did. The next morning, we woke early and made the short drive to the rim of the Grand Canyon.

Upon arrival, I didn't want to waste time looking for accommodation, so we paid the price and booked a cabin for two nights at the Bright Angel Lodge. What a perfect spot! We spent the next two days hiking the rim and Bright Angel and South Kaibab trails. The size of the canyon is something that cannot be described, only experienced. Eventually, we made our way to the North Rim for more hiking, and we booked a flatwater raft experience through the canyon. Simply stunning. Too soon, it was time to start the trip back home.

Neither Nadia nor I looked at a map as we started the trek back to Vancouver; we just knew to head north. We hiked in Bryce Canyon and picnicked in Zion National Park before heading back to Kanab, Utah, for the night. We had one day left of the trip and a 20-hour drive ahead of us, so we went to bed early. On the last day, we were in the car by 5 am for a very long day. Swapping off the driving duty and only stopping for gas and a quick pee break, we arrived in Vancouver around 1 am, and I dropped Nadia off at her house.

At this point in my life, I had never spent so much time with one person, but I was grateful that we managed to take the trip together. We became good friends and continued to hang out and do fun and crazy things together until I eventually left work. Unfortunately, over time, I lost contact with my friend, but the trip still remains one of my fondest memories.

The End

I hope you've enjoyed reading about my less-than-perfect vacations, and I sincerely hope that I was able to give you pause to rethink your misfortunes on your own trips.

I'm not sure where I'm off to next, but one thing I do know is that my trip will most likely be less than the perfection I'm seeking, but I suspect I'll have an entertaining story to tell.

If you have your own story that you would like me to know about, please don't hesitate to reach out at www.michellefedosoff.com

Acknowledgements

The creation of this book would not have been possible without the hard work and support of Vivienne, Julie, Stuart, Natasha, Rebecca, and all of the hardworking team members at Ultimate World Publishing. Thank you for pushing me.

Thank you to all my friends and family who love and support me and continue to travel with me, knowing they may end up in my next book. Love you all.

About the Author

Michelle is a writer and award-winning photographer who has traveled to 13 countries and counting. She travels solo, with her friends, family, and dog, Buddy.

While traveling, she's always on the lookout for the unusual and has braved street food in India, eaten haggis in Scotland, released turtles in Mexico, and gone on a grizzly bear safari in Canada.

She's a gifted storyteller and can often be found entertaining her friends and family with stories of everyday funny events, both at home and while traveling.

Her travel stories and photography have been published in several online and in-print magazines, and she's a guest speaker on Big Blend Radio.

Sites and Bites

As she continues to travel the world and share her adventures, she hopes to inspire others to step out of their comfort zones and find adventure.

www.michellefedosoff.com

Notes

Sites and Bites

Notes

Printed in the USA
CPSIA information can be obtained
at www.ICGtesting.com
JSHW080751071124
73089JS00004B/19